THE GREAT CRO

PARTHIAN

THE GREAT CROWD ROARS

a selection of the best Welsh football writing

EDITED BY
Gareth Williams

Parthian
The Old Surgery
Napier Street
Cardigan SA43 1ED
www.parthianbooks.com

First published in 2012
© The Authors
Introduction © Gareth Williams
All Rights Reserved

ISBN 978-1-908069-65-8
Published with the financial support of the Welsh Books
Council.

Cover design by Marc Jennings
Cover photo: photolibrarywales.com
Typesetting: www.littlefishpress.com

Printed and bound by Dinefwr Press, Llandybie, Wales.

Contents

Writing Welsh soccer

In 2007 I edited for the Library of Wales an anthology of Welsh sports writing. Unsurprisingly it was called *Sport*. The surprise, to the unsuspecting, came in the quality of the writing it contained; it was well received and has been several times reprinted. Its intention was to offer a sporting smorgasbord – from motor racing to rugby, cnappan to cricket – varied enough to revitalise the most jaded literary palate. Naturally soccer featured strongly, the third most substantial section after rugby and boxing, though not strong enough to satisfy the more rabid footie followers who probably share the view of one of Gwyn Thomas's characters that 'the oval ball is the symbol of deviousness. A round candid ball and no pawing of bodies, that's the honest English way'. But the 'English way' is a Welsh way too. The idea for this collection starts there.

Arguments will always rage as to whether the 'national' (i.e. Welsh) game is played with a spherical or an oval case of inflated leather. Beyond argument is the fact that so far this century the success of our two premier soccer clubs has by far eclipsed the dismal record of their regional rugby counterparts. The brilliant success of the Swans in reaching the Premiership, following hard on the Bluebirds' two recent Wembley appearances, demands that Welsh soccer's romance and rough rivalries, past and present, be celebrated by the best XI we can put out. This is it.

The title comes from Dannie Abse's poem 'The Game'. Dannie has written so evocatively about what Americans call 'soccer-football' that I make no apology for including him twice. There is other good writing here too.

Gareth Williams

THE
GREAT
CROWD
ROARS

DANNIE ABSE

The Game

Follow the crowds to where the turnstiles click.
The terraces fill. Hoompa, blares the brassy band.
Saturday afternoon has come to Ninian Park
and, beyond the goal posts, in the Canton Stand
between black spaces, a hundred matches spark.

Waiting, we recall records, legendary scores:
Fred Keenor, Hardy, in a royal blue shirt.
The very names, sad as the old songs, open doors
before our time where someone else was hurt.
Now, like an injured beast, the great crowd roars.

The coin is spun. Here all is simplified,
and we are partisan who cheer the Good,
hiss at passing Evil. Was Lucifer offside?
A wing falls down when cherubs howl for blood.
Demons have agents: the Referee is bribed.

The white ball smacked the crossbar. Satan rose
higher than the others in the smoked brown gloom
to sink on grass in a ballet dancer's pose.
Again it seems we hear a familiar tune
not quite identifiable. A distant whistle blows.

Memory of faded games, the discarded years;
talk of Aston Villa, Orient, and the Swans.
Half-time, the band played the same military airs
as when the Bluebirds once were champions.
Round touchlines the same cripples in their chairs.

Mephistopheles had his joke. The honest team
dribbles ineffectively, no one can be blamed.
Infernal backs tackle, inside forwards scheme,
and if they foul us need we be ashamed?
Heads up! Oh for a Ted Drake, a Dixie Dean.

'Saved' or else, discontents, we are transferred
long decades back, like Faust must pay that fee.
The night is early. Great phantoms in us stir
as coloured jerseys hover, move diagonally
on the damp turf, and our eidetic visions blur.

God sign our souls! Because the obscure staff
of Hell rule this world, jugular fans guessed
the result halfway through the second half,
and those who know the score just seem depressed.
Small boys swarm the field for an autograph.

Silent the stadium. The crowds have all filed out.
Only the pigeons beneath the roofs remain.
The clean programmes are trampled underfoot,
and natural the dark, appropriate the rain,
whilst, under lamp-posts, threatening newsboys shout.

from *Tenants of the House* (1957)

GERAINT H. JENKINS
Leigh Richmond Roose

It is one of the commonplaces of sport that a goalkeeper is rather different from the rest of mankind and certainly from his fellow footballers. From the days of William ('Fatty') Foulke, the gargantuan Shropshire-born international custodian who used to get his retaliation in first by waddling naked into visiting dressing-rooms to intimidate opponents and referees, to Rene Higuita (El Loco), the eccentric Colombian keeper whose surges upfield and scorpion kicks passed into folklore, goalkeepers have taken pride in being deemed a breed apart. Arguably the most gifted superman of them all was Leigh Richmond Roose, the 'Prince of Goalkeepers' in Edwardian Wales, whose *curriculum vitae* was a thing of wonder. No other member of the Welsh Hall of Footballing Fame can claim to have sat at the feet of the father of modern science fiction H. G. Wells, won nineteen of twenty-four international caps playing alongside the incomparable 'Welsh Wizard' Billy Meredith, represented clubs as diverse as Stoke, Everton, Sunderland, Huddersfield, Aston Villa, Woolwich Arsenal and Celtic, entertained the music-hall star Marie Lloyd, and prompted the dry-as-dust Welsh historian Thomas Richards to refer to him in awe as 'this wondrous Hercules' ('Yr Ercwlff synfawr hwn').

Born on 27 November 1877, Roose was a native of Holt, near Wrexham. His Anglesey-born father, Richmond Leigh

Roose, was a Presbyterian minister and the author of *The Five Senses of the Body* (1875). He sent his son to Holt Academy, whose prospectus offered 'a sound English Education, together with Greek and Latin, or German and French'. Under its principal, James Oliver Jones, discipline at the academy left much to be desired, and when the young H. G. Wells was appointed master in 1887 the menacing attitude of some of the older pupils unnerved him. While refereeing a football match on a wet Saturday afternoon, Wells fell on the muddy field and was severely kicked in the back by Edward Roose, Leigh's brother, and spent several weeks incapacitated with a ruptured kidney. Wells left shortly afterwards, but it may well be that his provocative independence and obsession with the bizarre fruits of science left their mark on Leigh Richmond Roose and that this prompted him to read science when he arrived at the University College of Wales, Aberystwyth, in 1895.

Although the 'College by the Sea' was not, as the embittered Goronwy Rees liked to claim, 'a theocratic society, ruled by priests and elders', the Nonconformist way of life was a powerful influence on staff and students alike. When R. Williams Parry, later to become one of Wales's most celebrated poets, confessed to Principal T. Francis Roberts that he smoked cigarettes and played billiards, he was asked: 'What other sins have you, Mr Parry?' Most students worshipped regularly and the historian R. T. Jenkins recalled seeing Roose many times in his sober dark blue suit in the English Presbyterian chapel. However, since his father had failed to pass on the native language, Roose never darkened the meetings of the Celtic Society (Y Geltaidd), and wild horses would not have dragged him to the coy soirées and at-homes which figured so prominently in the social round of staff and students. He had the reputation of being a self-possessed, rather aloof loner. From time to time, however, he figured in tempestuous student debates, interjecting on one occasion 'at a speed of some 300 words per minute' in order to demolish the argument of a priggish Liberal, and, on another occasion, winning thunderous applause by vigorously opposing a motion that athletics was 'detrimental to the best interests of the nation'. In February 1899 he was persuaded to take part in a mock trial, 'The Ass and the Ass's Shadow: The Great Case of John Jones v. John Jones in the Shadow of the Ass'. Cast as a policeman, his sole contribution was to roar 'Silence in Court!', which he did with such panache and authority that many believed it was the highlight of the evening. Roose was also one of the few students who dared to twit the head porter, Sergeant Wakeling, a tragicomic Falstaffian figure who ruled the quad with a rod of iron and whose malapropisms provoked much private hilarity.

As a result, although 'Mond' Roose kept his distance from fellow students, he became an iconic figure. Women students adored him and flocked to sporting events in order to cheer on and flirt with their hero. Puerile rules and regulations designed to restrict the mingling of the sexes were ignored or circumvented at the Vicarage Fields where, summer and winter alike, Roose was the principal focus of attention. At cricket his superlative fielding more than compensated for his Tufnell-like batting (his average was 3.83 in 1898) and his bowling was brisk and lively. During the annual Sports' Day he basked in the adulation of his admirers, proving invincible at throwing a cricket ball and winning the shot putt, high jump and piggy-back events in May 1899. Only when other mortals fell below his high standards did he lose his composure. At a gymnastic display held in the examination hall, a dishevelled Roose failed to rally the Science team in a tug-of-war competition and was reported to have been 'uncertain whether to stand on his head or his feet'.

But it was as a brave, unorthodox, idiosyncratic and marvellously athletic goalkeeper that Roose gained his reputation as a genius. While playing for the College, he particularly savoured the bruising contests against the students of Bangor, and such was his prowess that Aberystwyth Town FC also captured his signature. Roose represented the 'Old Black and Green' on eighty-five occasions, and on 16 April 1900 he was carried shoulder-high from the field when Aberystwyth trounced the Druids 3–0 in the Welsh Cup Final. By the time of his departure from the College, the *Cambrian News* had exhausted its fund of superlatives in recounting the exploits of this extraordinary figure. Roose moved to London to train as a doctor at King's College Hospital, but although James A. H. Catton, who wrote under the pseudonym 'Tityrus', referred to Roose in the *Athletic News* as 'this eminent bacteriologist' he never qualified as a doctor and thus earned a living as an extremely expensive 'amateur' player for a host of illustrious clubs in the First Division of the Football League. He made 144 League appearances for Stoke in 1901–4 and 1905–8, helped Everton to reach the runners-up position in the League and the semi-final of the FA Cup in 1904/5, and during four seasons at Roker Park helped Sunderland to finish in third place in the League on two occasions. When the *Daily Mail* invited nominations for a World XI to challenge another planet, Roose was the undisputed choice as goalkeeper. His League career ended with Woolwich Arsenal in 1911.

... Like wicketkeepers, goalkeepers are born rather than made, and Roose certainly possessed all the necessary physical attributes. Standing 6ft 1in. tall and weighing 13st 6lbs, he cut an impressive figure and could both physically and literally look down on most of his fellow players. Roose's jutting browline, small intense eyes, well-groomed moustache (at least in his student days) and wide, powerful shoulders oozed authority and defiance. His phenomenal reach and huge hands – Thomas Richards referred to his 'prehensile grip' – enabled him to make saves which lived long in the memory. Moreover, his sharp eyesight, startling reflexes, competitive instinct and reckless bravery made him an extraordinarily daunting opponent. Goalkeeping is a demanding position and Roose's flamboyance should not blind us to his athletic and technical prowess.

Yet throughout his career (and even unto death) there remained an air of surprise and mystery about Roose. A repertoire of well-rehearsed, though sometimes impromptu, eccentricities were an integral part of the Roose legend. The fact that he was a middle-class amateur in a largely professional game did not mean that he played purely for pleasure, for his 'amateurism' was a token of his social exclusivity as well as a passport to financial gain as a roving 'guest' player. He expected, indeed demanded, extravagant expenses and lavish hospitality for his services. Often he would awaken public interest by arriving at the ground in a horse and carriage, which was followed through the streets by entranced young supporters. On one occasion he hired a special locomotive to transport him from London to Stoke, and charged the costs of the journey to the club. A born self-publicist, Roose knew how to add thousands to the gate. When Wales were due to play Ireland in March 1909, he arrived at Liverpool for the journey to Belfast with his hand heavily bandaged. He claimed that although two fingers were broken he would be fit to play the following day. His two closest friends, Billy Meredith and Charlie Morris (both from Chirk), were too streetwise to be taken in and, peeping through the keyhole of Roose's room in their Belfast hotel, they saw the great man remove the bandage and wiggle his fingers without any sign of discomfort. News of Roose's 'disability' spread like wildfire and on the following day, before a huge crowd, the Welsh goalkeeper played a blinder and Wales won 3–2.

Like many (perhaps all) goalkeepers, Roose was highly superstitious. His attire was strikingly different: he wore white sweaters, twin-peak caps and padded knee-bandages. Although he carried white gloves onto the field, he seldom wore them, preferring to catch and fist the ball with his bare hands. Like Neville Southall, his dishevelled appearance at the beginning of a game gave the impression that he had just completed another. He preferred to play in unwashed shorts and during his season at Everton it was noticed more than once that his pants 'carried about them the marks of many a thrilling contest'. He insisted on wearing another shirt (some claim it was the old black and green shirt of Aberystwyth Town FC) under his international jersey and he never allowed charwomen to wash it.

Whereas most goalkeepers in the Edwardian era walked on to the field of play, Roose used to run briskly, acknowledging the applause before pacing the goalmouth like a restless tiger.

… Even though the heavy brown footballs used in Edwardian days virtually became medicine balls in wet conditions, Roose could kick and throw them prodigious distances. On dry days he sent thumping kicks the length of the field and punched the ball well beyond the half-way line. According to James Ashcroft, an intelligent goalkeeper with Woolwich Arsenal, nothing gave a goalkeeper greater satisfaction than fisting the ball long distances: 'It is more than a sensation. It is an ecstasy.' But one suspects that Roose derived even greater pleasure from plunging headlong among flying feet and bruising bodies. 'Rushing the goalkeeper', particularly from corners, and heavy shoulder-charges were part and parcel of the game. But aggressive forwards held no terror for Roose and when, for instance, a scrimmage developed when Stoke met Arsenal it was 'all Lombard Street to a halfpenny orange that the Reds would score', only for Roose to emerge from the ruck with the ball clasped to his chest. Roose deliberately intimidated opponents with his fists and during his spell at Aberystwyth liberal quantities of Robert Ellis's celebrated embrocation for sprains, stiffness and bruises were required by chastened forwards.

Roose's physical presence was a powerful psychological advantage for his teams. Like Peter Schmeichel, he oozed confidence, filling the goal with his mighty frame and 'psyching' opposing forwards. He exercised a strangely hypnotic influence over hesitant strikers, forcing them to scuff their shots or blast them wide of the goal. He enjoyed taunting experienced international forwards, some of whom felt the full force of his fist in goalmouth mêlées. On his day, he was an extraordinary shot-saver. In his first international he saved a point-blank drive from six yards by trapping the ball between his knees. Crowds marvelled at his spectacular leaps across goal and his mysterious ability to change his body posture in mid-air. If contemporary accounts are reliable, the save which Roose made while representing Aberystwyth against Builth in the Leominster Cup in April 1897 was at least the equal of that made by Gordon Banks against Pelé at Guadalajara in the 1970 World Cup. Some of his most breathtaking mid-air saves were from penalties. When Thomas Richards, the son of a Cardiganshire cottager who became Wales's foremost authority on seventeenth-century Puritanism and Dissent, was persuaded by a fellow student to attend a memorable encounter between Aberystwyth Town and Glossop North End, a professional team from the Midland League, he was so intoxicated by Roose's performance that, many decades later, he was able to describe the match as if it had occurred the previous day. In a Cardus-like portrait, written in Welsh and entitled 'Gŵr o Athrylith' ('Man of Genius'), Richards depicted with subtle scriptural nuances an astonishing penalty save by Roose:

…one of the full backs committed an unforgivable foul in the penalty box; the harsh blast of the referee's whistle, his finger pointing to one of the most calamitous places in the purgatory of this life – the penalty spot. The heavy odour of death hung over this fateful spot: did you not hear a crowd of thousands suddenly become dumb mutes, did you not see the players standing in a half circle as if they were at the graveside… Everyone holding his breath. I have always believed that Roose grew to his full height as a man in the purgatorial crisis of a penalty, drying off the clay around his feet, washing away the dross which entered his character with the gold… Arthur's sword against the bare fist. Then came the signal; the ball travelled like a bolt from the foot of the penalty-taking forward,

and in the blink of an eyelid, revolution, a thump, and
the ball landed in the heather and gorse of the Buarth.

from *For Club and Country* (2000)

PETER CORRIGAN

Billy Meredith

Whether L. R. Roose would have continued playing had he survived the war is hard to say. Possibly Meredith's example would have encouraged him for Billy's career stretched well into the 1920s. He played his last game for Wales in March 1920, against England in London, when he was 46 years old and he was but a few months short of his 50th birthday when he played for Manchester City in an F.A. Cup replay at Cardiff in 1924.

His career was prodigious which ever way it is looked at. Some estimate he played as many as 2,000 games. More likely was the figure that he claimed of 1,568 of which 857 were League matches played in the 31 years between making his League debut in 1894 and when he eventually retired in 1925. Before he died in 1958 at the age of 83, Meredith was asked what he thought of Stanley Matthews, that other evergreen right winger whose brilliance challenged Meredith's. The reply was most complimentary until the famous Welshman concluded: 'But I do wish Stan could have scored a few more goals.'

And there was the great difference. Meredith scored 470 goals in his career and many were match-winners. But his record was unassailable from so many directions. He became the oldest player to play in the International Championship in that 1920 game against England which was his 48th appearance in the Championship.

Ivor Allchurch and Cliff Jones have amassed higher totals for Wales, while Billy Wright, Bobby Charlton and Bobby Moore have all passed the 100 mark for England – but no-one throughout the four home countries has played in as many Championship matches as Meredith. There were no official fixtures against foreign opposition in his day so the Championship was the only source of caps and even then he missed many games for Wales because of club duty.

He played for both Manchester clubs, he was with United between 1906 and 1915, and played for both in a F.A. Cup Final. As well as those two medals, he had two League Championship medals, two Second Division Championship medals and two Welsh Cup medals.

Later, when he kept a pub in Manchester and his customers drank thirstily at his stories about the game, he could be persuaded to lay out his medals and caps along the counter and, as he pointed out, the caps were all the same size – 6 and 7/8ths.

But there was frequent controversy over the number of caps Billy Meredith gained. Even he thought he had won over 50, but he was entitled to that confusion because the Football Association of Wales made a presentation to him in February 1920 in recognition of his 50th cap and he played for Wales once more after that.

The F. A. W., however, were misled. Although Meredith was selected to play against Ireland in 1899 his club refused to release him at the last minute and somehow his name stayed in the records as having played. His official total was 48, made up of 20 matches against England, 12 against Scotland and 16 against Ireland, and he also played in two 'victory' internationals against England in 1918 which are not recognised as official games.

By 1900 he was established both in the Football League and internationally as a winger of exceptional class. He had made his Welsh debut at the age of 20 in Ireland in 1895 where, despite being seasick on the voyage to Belfast, he played well in a 2–2 draw. On the following Monday they had to play England at West Kensington where, he said, 'I saw more top hats than I had ever seen in my life.'

England had an all-amateur team out that day and Billy met the famous C. B. Fry and W. J. Oakley, the latter giving him a hard time of it. 'He made me gallop that day. Once he kept shoulder to shoulder with me for half the pitch which was 150 yards long.'

The following year Meredith was included in the Welsh team which met England in the first soccer international ever played in Cardiff, and which as a missionary project was a disaster for England won 9–1, the legendary Steve Bloomer scoring five of the goals.

The South Walians who looked askance upon that performance probably didn't even notice the young right winger because Billy Meredith was not the sort of player to excite interest at first glance. His sparse, erect body was perched on legs so spindly they did not look capable of supporting a piano stool. His face was drawn and unremarkable apart from the eyes that were direct and challenging. Overall the impression he gave to the stranger was more likely to attract sympathy than admiration.

But once he started playing the transformation must have been staggering. He didn't have great speed but he had that vital quickness over the first few yards and those legs provided so much balance and manoeuvrability that he could take the ball past you in a telephone kiosk. Once in flight and free of immediate challenge he had hair splitting accuracy, whether placing a cross with great precision or letting fly with a shot that had surprise as its first ally and force as its second.

And all the time his teeth were champing on a tooth pick, deftly transferring it from one side of his mouth to the other as his feet and brain worked their miracles. Some thought the toothpick served some mystical, calming purpose but the reason was more basic.

When he worked down the mines he chewed tobacco constantly and carried on the habit when he went to play for Manchester City. But his dribbling must have been fairly fluent all round for soon the laundry were complaining at the state of his jersey front and he was kindly asked would he chew something else. He chose a toothpick.

By the time the Welsh F.A. bucked up enough courage to play in Cardiff again, which was in March 1900, Meredith was far better known. 'The finest right winger living' said the *Western Mail* in passing.

Wales borrowed Cardiff Arms Park for the occasion, which meant they had to play on a Monday because Cardiff R.F.C. were playing Newport there on the Saturday and even though the rugby hero of the day Gwyn Nicholls was not playing because of injury, there was a crowd of 10,000 for the game.

The F.A.W. were expecting 20,000 for the soccer international with excursions coming from all over the country. The *South Wales Echo* reported, somewhat haughtily, 'the kick-off has been arranged for 4 p.m. to allow the artisan classes to see the game without undue sacrifice of working time'.

Wales, dressed as they were in those days in shirts of white and green halves, took the field to a slight sprinkling of snow and within three minutes were a goal down. According to the reports they would have stayed that way had it not been for Meredith. He had gone very close with a shot from the touchline in the first half, but in the second half the following happened:– 'Morgan Owen gave Meredith a beautiful long pass and he dribbled prettily past Oakley and getting close to Robinson put in a drive which no man on earth could have stopped. The ball hit the crossbar and bounced off into the net amid immense cheering'.

The score remained at 1–1 and the crowd went away happy at having Meredith's greatness confirmed before their eyes. Had Roose been able to play they might have had a second hero to discuss, but one was enough to prove that here was a man, and here was a game, worth some attention.

from *100 Years of Welsh Soccer* (1976)

'A SPECIAL CORRESPONDENT'

Stirring Moments at Wembley, 1927

'Nineteen-twenty-seven – the year Cardiff City first won the Cup' That is how Welsh football history and, perhaps, some other history too, will come to be dated in the future. And no one who was present at Wembley on Saturday can easily forget the scenes or the singing, the tense anxiety of the closing minutes of the game, the great Welsh shout of triumph when the referee shrilled out the final and Keenor, captain of Cardiff City, followed by his men, went up to the King to receive the FA Cup, which, for the first time in its half-century of history, has been taken out of England.

The winning goal came when many of us had almost resigned ourselves to a replay. Neither side seemed to be playing sufficiently good, clever and finished football to win, or to deserve to win. Then the unexpected happened. Ferguson shot into the goal-mouth. The Arsenal goalkeeper caught it. Len Davies was not far off, but still far enough away to be no cause of anxiety. Lewis, the goalkeeper, had plenty of time apparently to clear. He bent to his knees to gather the ball, and in bending he turned away from Davies, who was racing up. Everybody expected to see him rise and get the ball away. Nobody really expected a score. The silence was tense all the same. Then Lewis fumbled – that is how it seemed to spectators in the stands: Cup-tie nerves, perhaps. It is said that the ball was spinning and was difficult to hold, and that may be, of course, the explanation. At any rate, we saw the ball slip out of his hands and roll, all too slowly, it seemed, towards the net. There were Arsenal shouts of dismay and Cardiff shouts of joy. Lewis tried to grab the ball. Too late: it had crossed the line. Len Davies was leaping high in the air; a leap of triumph. Lewis, a rather pathetic figure, went slowly into the net to get the ball. It was destined to be the winning goal, and Lewis, who had played so well, had seemingly let his side down.

When the great crowd, close upon a hundred thousand, realised what had happened, such a shout went up as Wembley had never heard before. The crowded tiers of the vast amphitheatre became a stormy sea of tossing, waving hats and blue and white favours. Everywhere people were standing up, shouting themselves hoarse. In the Royal Box the King was smiling. Behind his Majesty the face of Mr Lloyd George was wreathed in patriotic smiles. Behind him again Mr Winston Churchill was smiling over to his old colleague of Coalition days little messages of national congratulation.

The Lord Mayor of Cardiff, excusably forgetful in the circumstances of the decorum of the Royal Box, joined the throng in a demonstration of enthusiasm that has rarely been equalled on a football field.

When the shouting had ceased and the game was re-started, there were many who, on reflection, qualified their enthusiasm with sympathy for the Welshman who was keeping goal for the Arsenal. And let it be said at once that a misfortune which might have unnerved most players seemed only to stimulate the Arsenal to greater efforts and to make Lewis himself rise to great heights again and again to avert further disaster. Cardiff City's supporters lived through anxious moments in the last fifteen minutes of the game. There were keen, desperate attacks and thrilling saves. Experts may call the quality of the football poor, but there was no denying the tremendous pace, the eager attack, the stern defence...

At the start it seemed as if both sides were suffering from nerves. Arsenal were playing the better football – their passing was infinitely superior. Buchan was always in the picture leading attacks, and Hardy was always in the picture, too, breaking them up and making magnificent clearances. As the game proceeded the pace increased, and when Cardiff scored it gave them just the tonic and the confidence they seemed hitherto to lack. Desperately anxious and thrilling though the close was, Cardiff City were now clearly the winners and they played a sporting open game to the end. There was none of that futile, unsportsmanlike waste of time that has spoiled many a good match after the first score. Up to the very call of the whistle, both sides were striving hard, one to equalise, the other to increase its lead. And so, whatever the experts may say of the quality of the football and the nature of the goal, Cardiff City's victorious Cup Final will be remembered as amongst the most sportsmanlike and the cleanest on record.

It will be remembered, too, for many other things. Some will call it the singing Cup Final. If this community singing is persevered in, it will not be necessary soon to come to Wales to hear singing. For many hours before the game began the crowds waiting in the Stadium were singing, and as the people surged into the great amphitheatre the volume of sound increased until, when the King came in, the National Anthem went up with a fervour that recalled the heroic, loyal days of 1914. It was a great crowd of sportsmen, more than half red, perhaps a third blue and white, judged by the favours that were shown about, and a very large section neutral, but whether the warp and woof were red or blue the result was a web of happy, loyal sportsmen gathered to witness a great contest. Instinctively they all turned to the King after the National Anthem, and spontaneously they sang the old song of democratic greeting and good-fellowship, 'For he's a jolly good fellow'.

Then, as the crowds continued to pour in, favourite old hymns and songs were sung. As Welshmen we longed for 'Cwm Rhondda', with its thrilling, almost barbaric, beauty of swelling harmony, but 'Hen Wlad' satisfied our national pride; and most beautiful and wonderful of all was 'Abide with me', sung with all its pleading tenderness by ninety thousand people. Not even the thrills of the game, nor the shouts of triumph, can efface the memory of that great hymn sung by so many, and yet sung so tenderly. Let it not be said that the English are not an emotional race. The Welsh men and women in the crowd were moved as one expected them to be; but so were the English; and many an eye was dimmed with tears, the memory carried back, perhaps, to heroic days of peril and sacrifice and unfaltering trust.

The memory of this deep emotion stands out against a background of joyous festival. For the English Cup Final is much more than a great football contest – much more than the climax of the football year, the conflict between the two teams that survive the ordeal of the rounds. It is a tremendous festival, and this year to an occasion hitherto – with one exception, and that again Cardiff City – exclusively English was added the flavour of an international: something of the flavour of an England v Wales Rugby contest at Cardiff or at Twickenham.

From Wales the men and women went up to London in legions. All through the Friday night and the early hours of Saturday morning the streets of London were musical with Welsh hymns and songs. The leek and the daffodil were almost as abundant, worn as favours, as the City's colours. It was not merely a Cardiff City occasion. It was an all Wales occasion.

from the *Western Mail* 25 April 1927

DANNIE ABSE

City Supporter

In the authorised silence of the house, upstairs in my bedroom, long past the fidgety tick of midnight, I lie horizontal under the sheets, my head on the pillow. The curtains are drawn. My wife, inert, asleep beside me. I stare at the back of my eyelids. This is the Waiting Room of Sleep. Before I am called to the other side of the adjoining door's frosted window, something needs to inhabit the restless mind.

I confess that during those last wakeful moments which stretch and elongate with advancing age like shadows moving away from a night lamppost, I frequently summon eleven blue-shirted Cardiff City football players, along with three substitutes, into the now crowded Waiting Room to autograph Sleep's Visitors' Book. I have done so intermittently over many decades. Different players file in, one by one. All wear the Bluebird shirt. Some announce their famous names: Trevor Ford, John Charles, Mel Charles, Ivor Allchurch, all of whom played for Cardiff City in their declining football years.

What a pathetic confession! What a ridiculous obsession! Am I a baby needing a sort of dummy before I can fall asleep?

Here I am, a grown-up man, indeed an old man, still dreamily involved with a relatively down-and-out Division Three soccer team. More than that, I'm hungry for Cardiff

City news: who's asked for a transfer? Who's injured? Who's in, who's out? What happened to X and will Ryan Giggs really sign for Cardiff?

In recent years I have become friendly with Leslie Hamilton, the Cardiff City doctor. Sometimes, when the Bluebirds play in or near London where I spend three-quarters of my life, he invites me to join him in the directors' box and enjoy the backstage pre-match and half-time hospitality of the home side. Always first, though, a sighing admonition: 'You can't come like that, Dannie. You have to be suitably dressed.' The short-haired businessmen who populate the boardrooms of football are stuffily rank conscious. Some Saturdays I wear a tie.

I must irritate my friend, Dr Hamilton, not only sartorially. Because I want to hear the latest Cardiff City gossip, the behind-the-scenes misdoings and machinations, the comings and goings, the resignations and aspirations, the betrayals of the last manager, the style of the new one, I sometimes clutch Dr Hamilton's lapels and cross-examine him. He, alas, remains, as a doctor should, invincibly discreet. Or I display my own swanking medical knowledge and query the constituents of the team's pre-match diet or propose, 'Given the absence of joint changes on clinical and X-ray examination; given normal laboratory findings, maybe it's just a psychogenic arthralgia?' How often he diverts my penetrative suggestions or diagnoses by telling me that he met someone who writes poetry. 'One of the players?' I ask hopefully, remembering the forgettable verses of ex-Cardiff City centre-forward, John Toshack.

I learn more about happenings at Ninian Park by reading the *South Wales Football Echo* which I have sent to me at my London home all season. Even when I worked as Writer-in-

Residence at Princeton University, New Jersey 08540, USA for the 1973–74 academic year, I ensured that the pink newspaper regularly reached our rented home in Pine Street. I did not subscribe to the *Times Literary Supplement*, the *New Statesman*, the *Listener*, or the *Spectator*. I needed to keep in touch only with vital news.

More important, of course, than football chatter is watching the actual games. This I did and this I do for I am a season-ticket holder. I arrange my frequent sojourns in South Wales to coincide with Cardiff's home fixtures. If invited to give a poetry reading at Hereford or Hartlepool or Scunthorpe or any other sad Division Three town I scan the Bluebirds' fixture list to suggest a particular Saturday evening date so that I can be rewarded by watching my team play on that same away-day afternoon.

Once upon a youthful time I often shared a platform or stage at a provincial town hall, theatre, library or pub, with Laurie Lee. When we were offered a tandem gig somewhere in the United Kingdom it used to worry me that Laurie would consult his address book to see if he had a friend, for all I know a girl friend, in this or that town whereas I merely fumbled yet again for the City fixture list. Dummy. Dummy. Cider only with the Bluebirds and not a Rosie in sight. Were, and are, my priorities wrong?

'If you want to go, you're on your own,' insisted my seventeen-year-old brother, Leo.

'The *Echo* reckons they'll do better than last season,' I said, trying to persuade my big brother to take me to Ninian Park.

'They couldn't do worse.'

'They've eight new players,' I mumbled.

Almost a year earlier I had seen my first game. Leo had allowed me to accompany him to watch the Bluebirds play Torquay United. We had joined 18,000 jugular critics for that Division Three (South) match. City had lost only 0–1, so I was hooked!

That 1933-34 season when I first became a fan, Cardiff City's ponderous and awkward defence leaked 105 goals. If they, surprisingly, scored first then the headlines in the *South Wales Echo* would inevitably read BLUEBIRDS FLATTER TO DECEIVE. They finished bottom of Division Three and, pleadingly, had to seek re-election – their worst season in their history. Only a few years earlier, in the previous decade, the Bluebirds had been Division One League Championship runners-up, FA Cup finalists and FA Cup winners. But since 1929 they'd slid down the league tables as if greased. How are the mighty fallen! Tell it not at the Kop, publish it not in the streets of Highbury, lest the daughters of Swansea Town rejoice.

Though I had never seen them in their prime, they were still my heroes. When I kicked a football in Roath Park or a tennis ball in the back lane with villain Phillip Griffiths, I underwent a wondrous metamorphosis. I wore an invisible royal blue shirt and I responded to the name of speedy Reg Keating, the City centre-forward, a blur of blue, who was known to have once scored a goal. So I was very disappointed that on Saturday, 25 August 1934, Leo would not take me to Ninian Park because, as he said, they lost all the time.

So what? We always seemed to back losers in our house. We sided with the workers but the capitalists continued to water the workers' beer. Hadn't he, himself, taught me an alternative rhyming alphabet which began – A stands for

Armaments, the capitalists pride, B stands for Bolshie, the thorn in their side? We voted Labour, didn't we? But around our patch they always lost the elections. Leo drummed into me that the Red Indians were the good guys not the imperialist cowboys. It was true too: Saturday mornings at the Globe cinema, the cowboys, led by Tom Mix, always won. And hadn't I heard my mother muttering, shaking her head, 'Your Dad's a loser'? Was she, I wonder, only talking about horses and greyhounds?

It was my gentle and beloved father, though, who one Saturday of late August sunlight financed me – pennies for the tramcar journey, sixpence for the game – so that I could go ON MY OWN, for the first time, to Ninian Park. Still only ten years high, I set out on this daring expedition from our semi-detached house in Albany Road. I don't remember my farewell in the hallway but I bet my mother fussed and kissed me goodbye as if I were going on a trek to the North Pole.

An hour or so later I stood outside the Ninian Park stadium disconsolate. I searched through my pockets once more only to find the used tram ticket, pennies for my return journey and the handkerchief that my mother had pushed into my pocket before I left the house. The sixpence had vanished, the little silver sixpenny bit, so generously given to me despite business being so bad and Australia winning the final Test match by 562 runs, had become invisible.

All around me people filed through the turnstiles. Someone was shouting, 'Programmes, getcher programme,' and another fellow with a strange Schnozzle Durante croak attempted to sell the converging crowds this or that differently coloured rosette. There were policemen on foot and policemen on horses and amid all the whirl of movement a few stood lazily in front of an unhygienic-looking van whose owner in a white coat purveyed sizzling sausages and onions.

I listened glumly to the conversations of those standing at the van. I don't recall what they were saying. Perhaps they spoke fondly of the old days, of the great players who wore the royal blue shirt – Fred Keenor, Hardy, Ferguson and Farquharson, legendary figures before my time. I did not know what they were saying and soon, in any case, they moved off. No one loitered near the sausage van. Gradually the crowds in Sloper Road thinned out, to join the flat-capped masses swaying in the swearing terraces. I could hear the military band playing within the ground. I stood there, close to tears, knowing the misery of the world and that. Outside is a lonely place.

How did I lose that sixpence? On the way maybe, upstairs in the smoke-filled tram? Had I pulled the handkerchief out of my pocket and inadvertently sent the sixpenny bit rolling beneath one of the varnished wooden seats? Surely the pipe-smoking pensioner sitting next to me wasn't an evil, clever pickpocket? What would I tell them all when I returned home? Mama, I sat next to Bill Sykes.

A sudden, barbaric roar from the crowd within the stadium signalled that the teams had appeared from the tunnel. The game would soon begin. Still some stragglers hurried towards the turnstiles as I waited there, unwilling to retrace my steps down Sloper Road. Soon there were no longer any late-comers. I stood in solitary vigil listening to the crowd's oohs and resonant aahs, coming and fading now that the game had begun. I must have been crying for suddenly a gruff voice said, 'Whassermara, sonny?' He bent down, he was a policeman so he sided with the oppressors of the workers – Leo had told me. But when I confessed that I had lost my sixpence he advised, 'They let the unemployed in near the end of the game. They open the gates at the Grangetown end. You could slip in then, sonny.' He began to walk away. Then he changed his mind. He came back and gave me sixpence.

I joined the 20,000 spectators in Ninian Park who attended the first Division Three (South) game of the 1934–35 season. In the crowded Grangetown area between the goalposts I, umbilicus-high, tried to struggle through the massed supporters so that I could see my heroes. Suddenly, as was the custom with small boys, I was elevated by benign hands and passed down good-naturedly over capped heads to join other pygmies near the front. We beat Charlton Athletic 2–1 and Keating scored one of the goals. I thought you'd like to know that. Though we won those late summer matches we ended that season 19th in the league. As so often City 'flattered only to deceive'.

* * *

I am trying to recall in more detail how it used to be at Ninian Park before and after the old wooden Grand Stand, one evening in 1937, lit up with incandescent fury as it burned on and on and to the ground. The Canton Stand had not then been surgically abbreviated to render it safe to sit in. The Grangetown end, now open to the frequently raining Welsh skies, used to be steeper and higher and owned a long oblique roof. The Division Three crowds averaged 20,000 not the current 3,000.

Before the match a brass band, a uniformed platoon, would march around the touchlines, hoompa hoompa, as they played rhythmic military airs. Bollocks. And the same to you. Bollocks. A man pregnant with a huge drum would trail behind the platoon, while leading them an ostentatious conjurer would, at intervals, throw a somersaulting pole high into the air before catching it in his croupier-white gloves. How the crowd would have loved to observe that Clever Dick lose and drop it.

Just before kick-off the brass band would assemble outside the players' tunnel. When the team spurted on to the turf the band would strike up Cardiff's inappropriate, inanely optimistic, signature tune: HAPPY DAYS ARE HERE AGAIN. The crowd's welcoming shout to the emerging players would zenith to such decibels that the pigeons which, at one time, thrived under the roofs of the stands would fountain up and out and away.

In those sepia days before the war, season after season I, alone or with school friends, used to observe this pre-match ritual from behind the goalposts at the Grangetown end. Opposite, the length of the green pitch away, loomed the slanting roof of the Canton Stand on which was painted an advertisement for Franklyn's Tobacco. Beneath it, in the depths of the posterior darkness, small sparks of light would transiently appear here and there, above and below, to the left and to the right – evidence that the advertisement had been effective for the spectators were lighting up their pipes or cigarettes.

Before the commencement of the game, a flotilla of motorised wheelchairs carrying cripples of the First World War would settle below the wings of the Grand Stand behind the touchlines near the corner flags. By 1939 these odd, closed, ugly vehicles had become scarce but after the Second World War, out of the smoke as it were, in an unhappy reincarnation, new wheelchair vehicles appeared. Years passed before they vanished from the scene.

So often have I visited Ninian Park in fine, wet, or wind blown weather, have stood on the terraces, sat in the stands, been comfortable or bloody cold as I observed football fashions changing: the prolegomenon and the tactics on the pitch. Everything so different and so much the same. I see the brown ball become white, see it passed back to the goalkeeper who picks it up, though directed from his own teammate. I hear a referee's long whistle blow from a bygone year. How does the song go? I remember it well. And 1952 was a very good year: City returned (briefly, alas) to Division One and over 50,000 attended the final Second Division game against Leeds.

> Memory of faded games, the discarded years,
> talk of Aston Villa, Orient, and the Swans.
> Half-time, the band played the same military airs
> as when the Bluebirds once were champions.
> Round touchlines the same cripples in their chairs.

In those lean, utility, post-war years, before the introduction of floodlighting, fixtures began at 2.30 p.m. and the kick-off was even earlier mid-winter. Often, late in the game, the players in the smoke-brown, thickening gloom, would become, at the distant Canton end, anonymous astigmatic figures drifting this way or that without evident purpose. At the confusion of the final whistle, whatever the score – win, lose or draw – hordes of youngsters would invade the pitch. Some would bring on a ball and incompetently kick it into the empty Grangetown end goal with amazing delight, others would seek the players' autographs. They were hardly chased off. They had become part of the Saturday afternoon ritual.

Nor did one experience feelings of incipient threat as the crowds dispersed into and through the dusk of Sloper Road. Because money was scarcer, trains slower, motorways not yet built, away fans did not usually attend the game in numbers. The home crowd, being more homogeneous, shared the same gods (who failed them), chanted the same chorus. They belonged to the same defeated tribe.

Like many of the youngsters near the barrier behind the goalposts I held back at the end of the match in order to avoid the crush of the crowds converging through the big gates of the Grangetown end. How quickly Ninian Park became empty, forlorn, abandoned, as the unaccompanied small boys patiently waited there. Outside the lampposts jerked into luminous activity and somehow emphasised the oncoming darkness of a December night.

How many occasions did I see City lose; how often the thin, damp, Welsh rain descended in melancholy sympathy at lighting-up time as I quit the ground into Sloper Road to progress under the hoardings, to re-enter real life. '*South Wales Echo*, sir. Last edition. NAZIS ENTER RHINELAND. *Echo. Echo. Echo.*'

Silent the stadium. The crowds have all filed out.
Only the pigeons beneath the roofs remain.
The clean programmes are trampled underfoot
and natural the dark, appropriate the rain
while under lampposts threatening newsboys shout.

from *Perfect Pitch* (1997)

HYWEL TEIFI EDWARDS

Ninian Park, the first time

Soccer won my allegiance when I was a boy in the 1940s and
the memory of the post-war years when our communal fears
were exuberantly volleyed to oblivion in town and village
will never fade. For three intoxicating years my village,
Llanddewi Aberarth, its 'boys' having returned from active
service, actually fielded a side in the second division of the
North Cardiganshire League. Our first game was a 'friendly'
against a team of PoWs in nearby Llannon who had been
kicking a ball around for the better part of five years. We lost
13–1 and my mam-gu developed an immediate interest in
the Nuremberg Trials. It did not help that my father had
been a prisoner near Bremen for the better part of three
years.

On 21 October 1950, Aberarth AFC went to Cardiff to
see Wales play Scotland at Ninian Park. It was a trip worthy
of Dylan Thomas's word-spinning. I had only once before
been to Cardiff and that had been a Sunday school outing.
The trip to Ninian Park would be a venture of a different
kind. Perched on the parapet of the bridge we listened like so
many ravenous nestlings to one of our stalwart merchant
mariners as he warned us in unbiblical Welsh about the
predators who preyed upon innocents abroad in big cities:

'Bloody hell, watch out for the women in Cardiff! Hell's
bells, be prepared!'

'What do you mean, Rhys?'

'What do I mean? Listen boi bach, there are women in Cardiff who can play with your cock and take your ticket at the same time!'

Dear God! In the darker recesses of one's anticipation something stirred only to be instantly neutered by the terror of a lost ticket.

'Don't tell your lies, Rhys.'

'Lies, be damned! Listen boi bach, the last time I went to a match one old sow tried it out on me, but nothing doing, boi bach. This one of mine has been round the world!'

On our way home to an early bed we debated the veracity of our counsellor's anatomical evidence and decided that we would be well advised to disembark in Cardiff wearing a bathing costume over our underpants. And we made it to Ninian Park, giving females of all ages a wide berth and attracting compassionate looks as we crabbed along pavements, left hand thrust deep in trouser pocket, right hand clamped to right breast. There was a crowd of 50,000 to see the match and it was my first palpitating experience of being part of a nation exhorting its team to victory. I will never forget it. We lost, 3–1, but the boys from Aberarth had actually seen their heroes for the first time – Barnes, Sherwood, Tommy Jones, Burgess, Paul and Ford – Trevor Ford! We would re-enact their roles on the village schoolyard until the following October.

I did not see the inside of the Arms Park until 26 January 1952 when I took another bus trip with my schoolfellows to watch Hennie Muller's fearsome Springboks reduce the Barbarians to kindergarten stature as they defeated them, 17–3. A heavy snowfall in west Wales saw a few of us make the journey to Cardiff in Wellington boots, only to be met with bright city sunshine without a snowflake in sight. We trudged, ruefully rustic, to the stadium but quickly felt at ease as the Barbarians, with the exception of Bleddyn Williams, played as if they, too, were wearing Wellingtons. I relished it as another initiative experience but to my mind it could not begin to compare with the fervour of Ninian Park.

from *Heart and Soul* (1998)

RON BERRY

A Rhondda Derby

Betty had her eight-pound baby that particular Saturday morning, somewhere around two o'clock, consequently Gee-Gee lost a night's kip, but he galloped on to the Galed Blues' field like a Corinthian stalwart. We were a man short and Morley'd puffed around the fistful of spectators begging for a volunteer.

'What's it feel like being a father?' I asked Gee-Gee.

'She's a good kid,' he approved. 'Forgot about that cyst entirely when the time came. Doctor told her all along it was nothing to worry about.' He breasted down a volley from our goalkeeper, chipped it out to Nebo's son, and high pranced from the knees for a few moments. 'We can beat this bloody shower,' he said vindictively.

I said, 'Any idea what you're going to name the baby yet?'

'Aye, Elizabeth Ceinwen, Ceinwen after Betty's old lady. There's the whistle. Now listen, watch out for the through balls, Hughie. I'll be sending 'em on to you.'

'Did you hear about Tegwyn Thomas?' I said.

'Yeah, Betty mentioned something about her. In the pudding club, isn't she?'

'Joe Hart, he's the...'

'Burquish bastard he is,' Gee-Gee said. 'Gerrup in front, mun, the ref's waiting for you.'

On the whistle I pushed the ball to our inside left, who jinked like a drunken buzz-fly, banging himself into Galed

Blues' inside right. Straight off they had the ball, and I heard Morley Latham wailing at us to pass square. He was very nigh double rupturing himself over passing the ball square; he'd experienced this Continental type football via the telly box. But Albion All-Stars were eleven highly individual players with no genuine regard for team play. You take the average big-minded South Walian, he believes he can lick the world, he's better than George Bernard Shaw, or he could become richer than Clore if he really set his mind to it. Any brand of power or genius, the chopsy, industrialised South Walian knows it all. He'll work in the same pit or factory throughout his life, but he knows the lot. Irrepressible entertainers are the lowest of the low, and we come next.

Galed Blues sneaked a goal inside five minutes. They had the awkwardest right winger you'll ever see; he ran like a man with a stalk on, or as if he had a bunch of grapes between his legs. Gee-Gee tackled him and slid full weight over the touch-line, then this winger let our goalie crash into him, but he rose, climbing up space like a spider and all he had to do was tap the ball into the net. Our goalie bawled at Gee-Gee, accusing him of failing to mark his man.

'Man each, boys! Mark a man each!' appealed Morley.

Gee-Gee told the winger, 'You won't bloody-well do that again, butty.'

He didn't either, until the second half.

The game settled down to ding-dong from end to end, with the full-backs booting the ball anywhere off the twenty-five yard line. Our boys were marking all right, never a thought of trying something constructive, just mark, stop, slam into touch. And Galed Blues clung to their lead with the same tactics. At half-time I asked Gee-Gee about the through balls he was going to chip on for my benefit.

'This next half,' he said. 'We've got the bastards weighed up now. See that bloke on the wing? He's had his lot.'

'Oh aye, well done, boy,' I said.

But directly from the kick-off that awkward winger did another solo run. Leaving Gee-Gee grass-cutting on his knees, he worked the ball into the top left-hand corner. We were two down and Morley came waddling on to the field as if he meant to book the ref. They were all packed around him, demanding a foul on Gee-Gee, but clearly enough Gee-Gee and the winger tangled legs and Gee-Gee lost the use of his. Our side pulled together then, we had to because there were a few under-couraged ones in the Galed team, I mean obvious preeners who loved themselves in their football togs.

The ground was hard, and I still wore those Johnny Haynes boots, but I had to do a lot of chasing. My first offer came from a long high lob which deceived the Galed centre-half. We went up for it side by side, nothing resembling the leaping salmon or red deer you read about from John Arlott in *The Observer*, and I just managed to nod it back to our inside-right, Esger Rogers, who couldn't lose his first team place, not while his mother laundered our jerseys and shorts. A neat footballer, Esger, anyway. He worked the ball on a few yards, their left-back coming at him Zulu-wise, then Esger ran over the ball, blocking the full-back, and all I had to do was shove it past the goalie, Esger's goal as much as mine; he took a spew-maker in the taters from the full-back.

Right then, 2–1, Morley hurrahing up and down the touch-line like a co-ed's daddy. The game developed rough and boring afterwards. I shan't bother any more with it – we won 3–2. Esger scored, Gee-Gee got one off the spot, and

Nebo's son Dilwyn, he headed the false teeth of Galed's centre-forward. His upper dentures fell into his cupped hands like broken dominoes.

from *The Full Time Amateur* (1966)

JOHN TOSHACK
The Gentle Giant

The greatest player I've ever seen,
I'm sure you know the one I mean.
From watching him I learned so much,
A Gentle Giant with a subtle touch.

A Big Man with a secret gift,
He gave his colleagues such a lift.
In defence or in attack,
Nobody could hold him back.

It really was a marvellous sight,
To see him moving in full flight.
And when the ball was in the air,
Opponents used to stand and stare.
There wasn't a thing he couldn't do,
King John could score goals, stop them too!

Welshmen worshipped the ground he trod,
Italians treated him like a God.
But in spite of his undoubted fame,
His character remains the same.
Though all his goals are in the past,
The memories will always last.

from *Gosh it's Tosh* (1976)

TREVOR FORD

The Centre Forward

...All this confirmed my great faith in my style of play. It is fair, it produces goals and it pulls the crowds. Yes, I am fully conscious of the fact that many people roll up to the game just to jeer and hoot at Ford, but at least my style has the virtue of being positive; it is something strong and definite, not the milk-and-water stuff that is causing attendances to drop all over the country. To pull in the crowds and be a Soccer personality a centre-forward must have a lot. He must be able to let fly with both feet and from any angle. If he can't then he will never survive because a leader perpetually crowded by the stopper centre-half with little space in which to manoeuvre and no time to spare must have that something extra that notches the goals.

So let's give him equal facility with both feet. What else does he need? Speed – speed off the mark and the ability to put on a terrific burst; he must know no fear, he must have a powerful shot, and a high mobility with the Houdini flair for wriggling out of tight corners.

Anything else? – in my opinion, yes! He must be a worrier of the most pestilential sort, a bustler with utter disregard for the size of the full-back and the opinions of the hotheads on the bob bank, and a trier of the absolutely impossible. If, like me, he believes that there is a future in British Soccer, then he will have this fact burned into his brain; the thrills in Soccer are all there in the penalty box ready to be produced in all their noisy glory by the centre-forward who has all the qualities that I have spoken about. The mid-field moves, the clever approach work, the wing-to-wing passes are all very entertaining, but it is when that ball skids into the penalty area that the crowds begin to pant. That is when I go on the rampage hunting for a thrill for the crowd. They are goal-hungry, every man jack of them. They have come to see goals scored and it is my job to score them. If that includes charging the goalkeeper, either to get the ball from him or to bundle him and the ball over the goal line, then I am within my rights – and I am giving the public what it wants. Shoulder-charging is part of Soccer just as crash-tackling is part of rugby; take it away and we lose for ever that all-in action which the public demands – and has every right to expect from professional footballers. They pay the piper and I for one don't blame them calling the tune.

But so many men on the bob bank do not realize that if the shoulder-charge is banned from Soccer, then Soccer will die. Just as well take the hops from beer or the salt and vinegar from the late-night bag of fish-and-chips! Ban the shoulder-charge and this great game of ours would degenerate into a milk-and-water 'after you, my dear!' affair more like a leisurely, polite Sunday croquet engagement than a Saturday afternoon blood-warming trial of masculine strength and skill.

And another thing! A ban on shoulder-charging would allow considerably more scope to the snakes of Soccer – the really dirty players.

Who do I mean? – the crafty ankle-tappers who put men out of the game for a month, and openly boast of it in the dressing-room; the completely unprincipled players who hack blindly at a man's shins when the referee turns his back;

the roughs who lunge deliberately with their knees into a player's thigh muscle or groin; the back-slashers – players who kick up – backwards at a man coming from behind and rip his legs with a set of football studs. These are the snakes of Soccer; these are the men for whose blood the fans on the terraces should scream – but don't. And why? Because the snakes of Soccer are like the reptiles after whom I name them – they are cunning and vicious; they strike incredibly swiftly and at the right moment – when the referee is unsighted. So crafty are these rotten characters that their underhand tactics go unseen in the hurly-burly of the match.

It has always struck me as peculiar that most of the football snakes I have run up against are small weasel-like men. They have insufficient weight to use a shoulder-charge effectively, so they call on all the mean, dirty tricks they know – and get away with it.

Yet, because I am playing centre-forward and am right there in the glare of the goalmouth limelight, I am reviled and barracked when I go crashing and bashing my way through legitimately. Strange, isn't it? And how some of these snakes love to put me off my game! A few minutes after the starting whistle one of them will crack me on the ankle and grate, 'Take that, you Welsh – !' A couple of minutes later he'll give me another wallop and I know then that the stirring-up treatment is coming. The idea is to give me such a hammering early in the game that I progressively get angrier and angrier and go for someone a bit too fiercely. Then, because the Ford name is all too well known, an irate referee bounces over and snarls, 'Any more of that, Ford, and off you go!' I used to be a sucker for the stirring-up technique but I'm wise to it now. And I'm glad to say that there are a good many English League referees who are wise to it, too. Several have told me at various times, 'Just play within the rules as you have been doing, you have nothing to fear from us.'

I've tried all along the line to play within the rules and have run foul of referees on remarkably few occasions. Nevertheless, the bitter heartbreaking barracking and cat-calling I received from the fans when I was with Aston Villa and Sunderland forced me to the conclusion – sadly, I admit – that part of it at least was motivated by something that had nothing to do with football or any lack of skill on my part. Up there in the crowd were bigoted, prejudiced men and women who hurled vile abuse at me – merely because I am Welsh. I heard what they shouted and often my heart sank.

If these pig-headed people call themselves sports lovers then they do the name of sport a grave injustice. No real sportsman would allow his judgment to be warped by the fact that a player was born in Swansea and not Southsea. I am Welsh and proud of it; those who insult me because of my nationality merely betray themselves as intolerant, besotted followers of a game that is supposed to encourage all that is fine in man. Football deserves better supporters than that. And in the main – thank goodness – it has.

from *I Lead the attack* (1957)

DAVID FARMER AND PETER STEAD
Ivor

Across the land people knew of Ivor and for many years his name was largely synonymous with Swansea. 'Where are you from?' one would be asked, or more usually, 'Who do you support?' and the mere mention of 'Swansea' would be enough to elicit the immediate response: 'Ivor Allchurch'. Fans read about him in match programmes although, as had been implied, they hardly needed them as far as team line-ups were concerned. If Swansea Town were named on the cover then sure enough Ivor would be at inside-left wearing No. 10. But, as Sir Matt Busby once commented in a marvellous and entirely appropriate tribute, Ivor 'never needed a number on his back' for his polish and class were unmistakable. In fact almost everything about him was unmistakable. In those days footballers came in a far greater variety of physical shape and size and, indeed, one reason for the game's popularity in urban Britain was the way it catered for all the types to be found in the average terraced row, village or school class. Michael Parkinson once provided a useful guide for readers who could not remember those days when horribly ugly gnarled legs determined full-backs and wing-halves, frailty wingers, madness goalies, robustness centre-forwards, ranginess and thick skulls centre-halves and vision inside-forwards, with the distinct probability that the inside-left would be a consumptive intellectual. That final tag could never have been applied to Ivor but, even if he had appeared without a number, a crowd to whom he was a stranger would have spotted him immediately as the side's thinker, the ideas man, the passer, the genius, the player who would make things happen, and all that would have been obvious even as he ran out for the warm-up. Already he stood out, for there was a studied and yet natural elegance about the man, a refinement that was clinched by his unnaturally blond and wavy hair. Most fans saw him first wearing the white of Swansea, and that too invested him with a slightly unnatural and perhaps even priestly aura: there was, even before the kick-off, a presence and potential about this No. 10 which promised a new dimension – and a challenging one if he was in the opposing team.

In the game itself all that class and polish to which Sir Matt referred soon became evident. There was a rhythm and flow to Ivor's play that will become very familiar as his playing career is recalled. He was usually to be found just inside his opponent's half, either in or adjacent to the centre circle. On receiving the ball he would instinctively turn to shield it from any opponent before looking up and passing the ball immaculately either to a nearby colleague or, more usually to a waiting winger some thirty yards distant. Now this was prettily done and suitably applauded, but it was par for the course and almost every team in the land had a visionary who instinctively passed the ball in such a way as to convince the crowd that he could 'do it with his eyes closed'. But Ivor was more than a slide-rule passer. There was his control, his balance, his grace, his ability to dictate the pace of the game and to unlock midfield stalemates, but even more there was the way in which his whole body would suddenly be capable of changing the general rhythm of the game with just a sudden surge of energy that for him seemed utterly natural. That surge might involve a body swerve; that was one of his hallmarks and John Crooks once memorably referred to the way in which Ivor was capable of sending 10,000 people behind the goal 'the wrong way'. There could be quick one-twos with other forwards and then a short sprint followed by a surprisingly powerful and direct shot or a cruelly effective chipped shot, for he was a genuine finisher to a far greater extent that most mere 'passers'. If a goal had been scored he would turn quickly to get on with the game but there was always just a hint of a smile that conveyed real pleasure. If the shot hit the bar or narrowly missed he would simply shrug, gently flicking out his lower arms as the crowd shared his sense not so much of the game's frustrations as of its exhilarating tension. Every game was like this with no dissent, no anger, just a recital of skills within the shape and form of the team game that had its own course to run. Some games were won, others were drawn or lost but always there was the rhythm, the expectation, the moments of sheer delight, the poetry. Watching Ivor play was a confirmation of how life, however humdrum, allowed instances of utterly natural grace and excellence.

from *Ivor Allchurch, MBE* (1998)

HUW RICHARDS

Inter-City Rivalry

It is a truth universally acknowledged, at least if one's universe starts west of Bridgend, that the single good thing to have come out of Cardiff is the road to Swansea. Our capital city was recently branded by Swansea's *South Wales Evening Post*, in a headline making up in pungent expression of local opinion what it lacked in linguistic elegance, as 'a greedy city with a big mouth'. Amid the immense range of fissures characterizing modern Wales and exposed most graphically in the referendum on the creation of the National Assembly for Wales – north v. south, east v. west, Welsh-speaking v. Anglophone, Objective One v. Not Quite So Poor – none is more ferocious than that conducted, ever since the two communities emerged out of industrialization as the pole-stars of south-east and south-west Wales, between Swansea and Cardiff. Part of this rivalry is rooted in differences in character. Swansea's fortunes were built on metal-bashing, its cosmopolitanism as a seaport leavened by the influence of a hinterland which is consciously Welsh and not infrequently Welsh speaking. Cardiff's raison d'être was its location as entrepôt to the Rhondda coalfields, its character informed by rapid late-nineteenth-century immigration which brought it not only West Countrymen but the black and Irish populations who have made such an immense contribution to its sporting culture. But the real roots of dislike are common to anywhere two cities of roughly comparable size jostle for leadership, and the prizes that it brings – Manchester v. Liverpool, Newcastle v. Sunderland and Southampton v. Portsmouth come to mind. This battle has been won conclusively by Cardiff, taking not only newly created baubles such as capital status and the series of government agencies that go with it, but also prizes which were once shared – international rugby in 1954 and county cricket in the later 1990s. If no one in Swansea ever truly believed that the city would get the National Assembly, the irony that Cardiff was this time awarded a prize against which it had voted added a further edge to the bitterness of rejection.

That rivalry is seen at its most visceral in sport, an outlet providing a notionally objective test of superiority. One reason why Glamorgan cricket did not fix a county headquarters at the time of its foundation in the 1880s was that matches between Swansea and Cardiff were noted for skullduggery and contested results, and the club had no desire to import the quarrel. Wilfred Wooller, an adopted Cardiffian, wrote of the utter fury of a Swansea crowd when he stole victory at St Helen's with a late drop-goal some time in the 1930s. In football, a tangible air of fear and loathing hangs like malignant ectoplasm over derby matches at Ninian Park and Vetch Field, with the day's battles liable to be worked out ad nauseam in the letter columns of the local press by the one-eyed and the brain-dead of both sides. The match also has an inexplicable charm for satellite television's match-schedulers who fail to recognize that the quality of the football, however good or bad the teams in their other matches, is almost invariably lamentable. Like certain sexual practices, Swansea City v. Cardiff City matches should be performed in private with participation confined to consenting adults. And the rivalry also spreads into other matches. If some apparently inoffensive opponent is singled out for non-stop hostility at the Vetch Field, the likeliest explanation is that he is a former inmate of Ninian Park.

Yet there has been considerable interchange between the clubs over the years. This was underlined, perhaps unconsciously, in 'Only Sixty-Four Years', the poet Dannie Abse's beautiful essay on his lifetime as a Cardiff fan, in *Perfect Pitch*. Abse described how he would while away hours of sleeplessness by summoning up the images of great Cardiff players: 'All wear the Bluebird shirt. Some announce their famous names: Trevor Ford, John Charles, Mel Charles, Ivor Allchurch, all of whom played for Cardiff City in their declining football years.' Cardiff fans will have reacted to that sentence by considering the counter-claims of such as Fred Keenor, Alf Sherwood and Phil Dwyer. No Swansea City fan can read it without instantly remarking that the four names Abse conjures from Cardiff memories dating back to the 1930s all came from Swansea and all, but John Charles, first played for the Swans.

from *For Club and Country* (2000)

Gareth Williams

Gareth Williams has written and broadcast extensively on the sporting and musical history of South Wales. His books include the prize-winning *Fields of Praise* (with Dai Smith), *1905 and All That*, *George Ewart Evans*, *Heart and Soul – the Character of Welsh Rugby* and *More Heart and Soul* (both co-edited with Huw Richards and Peter Stead), *Valleys of Song: Music and Society in Wales 1840–1914*, and *Sport*, an anthology of Welsh sports writing. His most recent book is *Wales and its Boxers – the Fighting Tradition* (co-edited with Peter Stead). He sings with the Pendyrus choir and is Emeritus Professor of History at the University of Glamorgan where he was Director of the Centre for Modern and Contemporary Wales.

The Authors

Dannie Abse (b. 1923) prize-winning poet, novelist and doctor.

Ron Berry (1920–97) Rhondda-born novelist and writer.

Peter Corrigan (1935) sports journalist and historian of Welsh soccer.

Hywel Teifi Edwards (1934–2010) cultural historian, literary critic and professor of Welsh at University of Swansea.

David Farmer (b. 1920) emeritus professor of Henley, the Management College, and historian of Swansea's rugby and football clubs.

Trevor Ford (1923–2003) forceful centre-forward who scored twenty three goals in thirty eight games for Wales between 1947 and 1957.

Geraint H. Jenkins (b. 1946) historian and until recently Director of the Centre for Welsh and Advanced Celtic Studies in Aberystwyth. Currently writing the Swans' centenary history.

Huw Richards (b. 1959) historian, sports writer and free-lance journalist; author of The Swansea City Alphabet (2009).

Peter Stead (b. 1943) broadcaster, historian and cultural commentator; chair of the Dylan Thomas Literature Prize.

John Toshack (b. 1949) footballer, coach and poet; scored thirteen goals in forty appearances for Wales between 1969 and 1979.

PARTHIAN